ISBN 1 85854 806 3
First published in Great Britain in 1999 by Brimax
This edition published in 2000 by Brimax
an imprint of Octopus Publishing Group Ltd
2-4 Heron Quays, London E14 4JP
© Octopus Publishing Group Ltd
Printed in Spain.

Enchantment

By Gill Davies   Illustrated by Eric Kincaid

BRIMAX

Enter the world of Enchantment,
Step through the silver gate
To the land where sprites and fairies,
Hags and mermaids wait.
Explore the soaring mountains,
Lakes and forests deep,
Stormy seas and snowscapes,
A haunted castle keep.

Enter the world of Enchantment,
Step through the arch of gold
To the land where spells are made
And ancient tales are told.
Bring courage in your heart
For there are dangers here to brave:
Sorcerers and serpents,
Fiery dragons in the caves.

Enter the world of Enchantment,
Step through the mirror glass
To a land that holds you spellbound
As wraiths and goblins pass.
Sing with feasting elves,
Dance where the demons fly,
Enter the world of Enchantment
Before the chance slips by...

Wishing

I wish I had a wishing well,
I wish that I could cast a spell,
I wish I had a wand like fire,
Transformations to inspire.

I wish the fairies in my head
Were dancing on my hand instead;
I wish on elfin wings I'd fly
To dance with stars in velvet skies.

I wish the wizard in my dream
Could take me where the caverns seem
Full of dwarves and burning torches,
Where the dragon's fire scorches.

I want enchantment to be real
And terror, too, I need to feel;
I don't want ordinary days,
I want to thrill and be amazed.

I want those tingles down my spine,
To see a ghost that might be mine,
As friends in peril I'm defending...
I want to have a happy ending.

The Water Sprites

The fairies who play by the waterfall
Are delicate water sprites;
They dive in ⁀littering river
In a graceful, dainty flight.

They swim with the fish to the water's edge
And then scramble out to ㄱy,
Before soaring up to race in the air
With a dragonfly.

They love to ride on the bubbles,
They giggle and splash and play;
Then they rest in a hammock of cobweb lace
Where the sunbeams slant all day.

The fairies who play by the waterfall
Have wings that are gossamer light;
They shimmer with glimmering rainbows
That dance to the tune of their flight.

Neptune

Neptune is the sea god
Who lives beneath the waves.
With a trident in his hand, he stands
Where shipwrecks find their graves.

Neptune has a fiery temper
That stirs up screeching gales,
His terrifying anger turns to
Storms that swamp the whales.

His roar can cause an earthquake,
Which shakes the distant land;
His hair streams out like fire as
He stamps the rippled sand.

The dolphins gather round him,
Gazing up in awe,
As Neptune makes a tidal wave
Crash upon the shore.

Sea Serpent

The sea boils like soup
As coils writhe and unloop,
Rising up from the weeds deep below;
Fanged jaws are steaming,
Sliding scales gleaming,
A slimy head sways to and fro.

His neck cranes about,
Red-ringed eyes gazing out,
As he searches for something to eat;
But the ships that he sees
Seem as tiny as peas,
As the fleet beats a hasty retreat.

He glides off to the west
And discovers a nest
Of screeching orcs in a cliff hollow;
His jaws open wide
And the orcs slip inside
In one single, slippery swallow.

Under water he dives,
As his loops twist and writhe,
Propelling him on at full speed.
Down below in the dark,
He digests a huge shark,
Then slithers back into the weed.

Mermaids

They are racing through the water,
Playing in the sea,
Splashing through the white-capped waves
As they laugh with girlish glee,
Eyes dancing with excitement,
Wild and beautiful and free.

At last they rest, with mirrors raised,
And comb their silken hair,
Beckoning with silvery arms
To lure the sailors where,
Hearing songs that so enchant them,
They forget the dangers there.

So beautiful, so treacherous;
So innocent each glance,
Ships steer towards their loveliness,
Caught in a rapturous trance,
To seek a mermaid bride,
Or on jagged rocks to dance.

Haunted Castle

In a wild and craggy chasm
Deep with shadows in the night,
The moon slips up above the rocks
And casts an eerie light.

The stones seem to slide and melt
As they suddenly swell and grow,
To rise up as a haunted castle
With its windows all aglow.

Ghostly figures leave their dungeons,
Vampires leave their coffin lair,
To fly among the bats,
With cobwebs in their hair.

Clouds twist into misty faces,
As spectres swirl their capes;
Now the night is filled with fear,
And haunting, shadowy shapes.

The Sorcerer

The sorcerer is more ancient than time itself,
With terrifying, glittering eyes;
His cloak flashes mystically with stars and moons,
He stirs his potions with a twisted spoon,
Chanting, ranting incantations, making strange, wild cries.

The sorcerer stirs magic in a secret tower,
With his white hair flowing to the ground;
As the tower seems to tremble, quiver and shake,
Tremors crack the ground and ripple through the lake,
And lightning flashes all around.

The sorcerer can understand many, many things,
Magic and mystery are flashing in his rings;
Time is not an issue - he can twist it to and fro,
Making yesterday tomorrow and history come and go,
Then flying to the future, his cloak spread out as wings.

The sorcerer is more ancient than fact or fate;
He has powerful, glowering eyes
To penetrate and generate what is in your mind,
Leading to adventures where crystal pathways wind
And mountain peaks are piercing the skies.

Hags

Out of the deep, dark forest sliding,
Broomstick riding, tree-top gliding,
Cobwebs catching, moonbeams snatching,
Secret spells the Hags are hatching.

With wild cackles, flying past,
Shadows on the moon they cast;
Silhouettes of toothless crones,
Thin as twigs and dry as bones.

"I've snared a bat!" shrills one foul Hag,
Whilst one puts spiders in her bag.
"Firelight I've caught!" her sister screams,
"And now I'll steal some children's dreams!"

Home they swoop past yawning graves,
Back to sleep in forest caves,
To toss and snore in crawling rags;
A putrid heap of steaming Hags!

The Enchanted Forest

There is a deep, enchanted forest,
Long ago from dreams it grew,
Breezes whisper sweetest lullabies
And the branches beckon you.
But then the wrinkled trunks of trees
Turn to faces as you stare,
And in the night the forest eyes
Are gleaming everywhere.

Wolves and dragons prowl the forest,
Out of caves the bats come flitting,
While in pretty, sunlit glades
On toadstools gnomes are sitting.
In the deep, enchanted forest
You can hear harebells ringing,
And gushing streams lead where
The rushing waterfalls are singing.

There are fairies in the forest,
And wicked witches too.
White-haired sorcerers are stirring
Secret magic in their brew.
There are princes and woodcutters,
Princesses, happy and forlorn...
For this deep, enchanted forest
Is where fairytales are born.

Goblins, Imps And Demons

Goblins, imps and demons
Are the mischievous, capering folk,
Hobnobbing in the forest dark
Where twisted branches poke.
As imps dance round the toadstools,
Night's creatures come to peep,
To watch in flickering lantern light
The goblin shadows leap.

They thump and they stump,
They jump and they bump,
They point and they pry,
Shaking fists at the sky;
They sneer and they leer,
They jeer and they cry,
Pouncing and bouncing,
Feet flying high.

But goblins, imps and demons
Are as secret as can be,
So if you spy their night-time capers,
Do not ever let them see...
Or they'll dance into your nightmares
And never set you free.

The Snow Fairy

The fairy who wakes in the winter
Wears a lacy, snow-white gown;
Ice crystals frill the hem
And glitter in her crown.

Her wand is frosty silver,
Icicles crown her sleeves,
She dances through the tree-tops,
Dusting sparkle on the leaves.

The white rabbits are her friends;
They hop up on her knee
For a cuddle in the snow
And some fairy company.

She kisses every snowman,
And holds the rivers back from flowing,
Then skates upon the lake
Until her face is glowing.

She sleeps among the mistletoe
Or in a Christmas rose,
Covered in a feathered mantle
And with snowdrops at her toes.

Jack Frost

Jack Frost is up to his tricks again,
Scampering through the night;
He gleams as the silvery moonbeams
Fill his icy fingers with light.
He traces patterns on the windows,
Crystals sparkle there and shimmer,
Then glitter flows out from his toes
Until the frozen rooftops glimmer.

He has frosted the edges of the hedges.
He has painted the cobwebs white.
He has made every street and path
Glint with a twinkling light.
Then he flies back up to the stars again,
Empty and dark and still,
To rest until he's filled with ice
When he dances back over the hill.

Midsummer Queen

The fairies are holding a Midsummer Ball
Beside the shimmering pool;
They are all in their finest gossamer gowns
And glowing like precious jewels.

It's the night for granting wishes,
So the woodland creatures are there
In their finest fur and feathers
And with flowers everywhere.

The Queen of the fairies arrives in a barge,
All golds and garlands and silk.
It is pulled by majestic swans
As snowy white as milk.

The orchestra strikes up music,
Serenading the beautiful Queen,
As moon beams caress the lake
Until its satiny ripples gleam.

Dancing and feasting beneath the trees
That glow in the lantern light,
The Midsummer Queen grants many a wish
On this magical midsummer night.

Dragon

Dragon, Dragon breathing flame,
Your livid nostrils pulsing smoke,
Your heavy scales all silver glow,
Pulsating slowly to and fro,
As treasure trove you claim.

Coils surround the richest gems,
All stolen long ago;
Tenderly your tail enfolds
Caskets, goblets made of gold
With ruby crusted stems.

Your calloused head surveys the mound,
Ancient helmets, shields and rings,
Secure in there within your care;
No robber dare invade your lair,
Deep in that underground.

Searing, breathing, scorching sighs;
Oh, Dragon, you are waiting!
Powerful wings and fearsome claws,
Loathsome ripping, dripping jaws,
And armour-lidded, staring eyes.

Wraiths

High up in the icy mountains,
Where pathways zigzag like a snake,
Lies a hidden secret,
A forgotten, haunted lake.
Fathomless it plummets,
Hung in mountain-sides so steep;
Where, as silent as the shadows,
From the deep, the phantoms seep.

Water wraiths like mist,
Billowing like shrouds,
Rise up from the surface
In an eerie, writhing cloud.
They swirl up in a spiral
To fill the gusty sky,
Before flying down the mountains
To torment and terrify.

Twisting round the forest trees,
With the winds they wail;
Then racing through the snow
Leave a strange and slithered trail.
Eyes shine in the darkness,
The mist takes their ragged form,
They are patterned in the snow
And shrieking in the storm.

A Leprechaun

To be sure, I am a leprechaun,
Dressed in emerald green;
As merry a fellow as you could meet
And the smallest you have seen.

I've a cocked hat on my head, that's fine,
And an apron small and neat,
And I'm busily hammering shoes and brogues
For the daintiest elfin feet.

There's a crock of gold I'm hiding,
Don't you dare to steal it away;
I'm takin' it down to the rainbow's end
To bury it there today.
I shall hide it well and deep, I shall,
But if you should spy me there,
I shall vanish the minute you blink, with a wink,
With the rainbow, into the air.

To be sure I know many a trick to play,
And I'm as old as the old oak tree;
Small to the measure, but clever with treasure,
I'm a leprechaun, that's me.

Phoenix

Large as an eagle, red and gold,
The Phoenix is born of fire.
Spreading its wings, dancing as the flames
Turn to dust from its funeral pyre.

Oh, fabulous bird
With your melodious cry,
Worshipped by Egyptians
Beneath the desert sky,
Living for five hundred years,
Or more, before you die.

Sweet smelling boughs and spices
Make up your nest to burn,
So that another Phoenix
Can be born to take his turn.

Oh, fabulous bird,
Like the golden sun you blaze,
Splendid in your magic
Made of fire, to amaze,
Each feather like a flame
Haloes your eternal gaze.

The Feast Of The Elves

The King of the Elves is holding a feast,
It will last for a night and a day;
As the elven folk sing of adventures,
A beautiful harp will play.

Wine sparkles in goblets of silver,
Fruit flows over plates of gold;
As the firelight flickers the hall is filled
With laughter and tales retold.
Tales of battles with ogres and demons,
And dragons the elves have slain;
While the elves dance a rollicking jig,
Tapping their feet to a merry refrain.
Then the elven music grows sweeter still,
Like a flute on a flowery hill,
Like the ringing of bells and birdsong,
Till slowly all grows still...

The guests, made heavy with slumber,
Close their eyes in a dream-filled haze.
Enchanted, they sleep deep magical sleep,
And now only the firelight plays.

The Underworld

Deep below the ragged mountains curtained stalactites hang;
The dwarves are digging for gold, lit by a burning brand,
In caves with frozen waterfalls,
In a secret and shadowy land.

This is the gloomy Underworld where trolls and monsters lie;
Along the cavernous corridors echoing voices cry,
As the blackest of lakes unfurls
With ripples that surge and sigh.

A skeletal figure is waiting, waiting to row you now,
In a boat made of waxen ribs with a skull at its bony prow;
A great cloak hides his face...
The boatman makes a sweeping bow.

Do not step into the boat! Do not take his proffered hand!
Do not cross that black expanse to that shore of sifting sand!
For this is the Underworld
Where only the spirits can land.

Run back along those tunnels, run back to the world of light,
Around the misty marsh, to a home that is warm and bright;
Leave the mountains to guard their spirits,
And the will o' the wisp to the night.